THE
MIGHTY WARRIORS

DWIGHT
DAVID
EISENHOWER
The
Warring Peacemaker

by
ALLAN CARPENTER

Rourke Publications Inc.
Vero Beach, Florida 32964

EDITORIAL ACKNOWLEDGMENTS
Illustrations
WESLEY KLUG
Assistant to the Author
and Indexer
CARL PROVORSE
Typography by
LAW BULLETIN PUBLISHING COMPANY

Published by ROURKE PUBLICATIONS, INC.,
Vero Beach, FL 32964

Library of Congress Cataloging-in-Publication Data
Carpenter, Allan, 1917-
  Dwight David Eisenhower, the Warring Peace-maker
  (The Mighty Warriors)
  Bibliography: p. 107
  Includes Index.
  Summary: Chronicles the life and career of the West Point graduate who became a World War II commander, army chief of staff, head of the Nato armies, and the thirty-fourth President of the United States.
  1. Eisenhower, Dwight D. (Dwight David), 1890-1969—Juvenile literature. 2. Presidents—United States—Biography—Juvenile literature. 3. Generals—United States—Biography—Juvenile literature. 4. United States. Army—Biography—Juvenile literature. [1. Eisenhower, Dwight D. (Dwight David), 1890-1969. 2. Presidents. 3. Generals] I. Title. II. Series. E836.C37 1987 973.921'092'4 [B] [92] 87-9594 ISBN 0-86625-328-9

Previous pages, "Old Barn," a painting by Dwight D. Eisenhower.

CONTENTS

Contents continued on page 7

Dwight, D. Eisenhower, General of the Army, official portrait.

Contents Continued

Appendix

The little boy who began to learn about "war" by defeating a big bird, opposite, became the supreme leader of the greatest military force ever known. The climax of that career was the decision made by Dwight D. Eisenhower to activate D-Day and send millions of men into the final stages of World War II in Europe, as shown in this illustration by Wesley Klug.

Chapter One

WAR WITH A BIG BIRD

In the 1890s, life in Kansas was completely different from today. Wagons and carriages pulled by horses were the only means of getting around the town and countryside, except for walking. A trip on a train was a real adventure.

One Kansas boy had his first train ride when he was nearly five. He went to visit relatives on a farm near Topeka, Kansas.

On his first visit to the farmyard, he walked toward a group of geese. Suddenly, a gander came rushing toward him, flapping his wings and hissing fiercely. Geese can be quite fierce. Even today they are sometimes used as guard animals. The boy turned and ran back to the house. Every time the boy tried to go out into the yard the gander attacked.

The Eisenhower family home at Abilene, Kansas, as it looks today. Here Ike's mother and father provided for the most prominent of their six sons an extraordinary understanding of people and how to handle them and instilled in him a desire to live a full life.

Finally, his uncle made a "weapon" for him out of an old broom. He told the boy how to swing the broom and keep the gander away. The next time the gander attacked, the boy yelled back. He ran toward the attacking goose, swinging the broom. The gander gave a squawk and ran off. The boy was master of the barnyard.

In a way, this little "war" with a big bird might be considered Dwight Eisenhower's first military lesson. Much later he wrote that from this experience, "I quickly learned never to negotiate with an adversary except from a position of strength."

Chapter Two

LIFE IN ABILENE

Dwight David Eisenhower was born at Denison, Texas, on October 14, 1890. So Texas is his birth state. However, his parents moved to Abilene, Kansas, when Dwight was only one year old. So Kansas also claims him as its own.

His father, David Jacob Eisenhower, held a very respected place in the community; because of his great honesty, he was especially admired by everyone in the area. Dwight learned much about character and integrity from his father.

His mother, Ida Stover Eisenhower, always called him Dwight. However, before he was very old almost everyone else was calling him Ike.

Many of the lessons of everyday life were learned from his mother. When Ike was ten years old, his older brothers, Arthur and Edgar were

Ike's bedroom, as restored in the family home. Here a happy little boy grew up to become a self-sufficient young man, ready to go to West Point.

Ike's parents bedroom has been restored at the family home in Abilene. It helps to illustrate the modest but comfortable way of life established by a sturdy father and a brilliant mother.

given permission to go out trick or treating. His father said Ike was too young to go out with the others. As the two brothers set out, Ike was so angry he began to strike out at an old tree with his fists, cutting his hands badly.

Ike said that his father decided the matter with a hickory stick and sent him to bed.

After and hour or so, Ike's mother came into the room where he was sobbing into the pillow. He felt the whole world was against him.

After she had sat quietly by his bed for some time, she told him about temper and the value of controlling it. She often quoted from the Bible, and this time she quoted a paraphrase of one of the Bible quotations:

"He that conquereth his own soul is greater than he who taketh a city." She showed him that hating someone or something was useless and only injured the person doing the hating. In her family, she said, Ike needed this lesson the most.

She treated and bandaged his battered hands, pointing out that he was the one who had suffered most by his anger.

"I have always looked back on that conversation as one of the most valuable moments of my life," Ike recalled.

When he was older and had a chance to think about it, Ike wondered how his mother had ever managed. She had to provide shelter and take care of all of the household chores of a family of eight,

The restored family home of the Eisenhowers at Abilene, Kansas, illustrates much about the background of the family, above, the parlor, below, the back parlor.

including the six Eisenhower brothers. Perhaps Ike gained from his mother some of his genius for organizing great ventures.

"Mother was by far the greatest personal influence in our lives," Ike wrote.

All the boys were taught to help with all the work of the family, and this helped them to understand the importance of whatever work they were doing. The future president learned how each member of the family could make a contribution to the family and develop character also. It was good to be wanted and needed.

Ike also learned lessons of a different type from his father. Before Ike was born, David Jacob Eisenhower had operated a store in Hope, Kansas. He hated farming so he sold the farm his father had given him in order to buy the store. Things went well for a while; then the farming country suffered drought and grasshoppers. The store's business dwindled.

Being kind hearted, the father continued to give his customers credit. When the store no longer could pay its own bills, the partner took the remaining cash, left town and was never heard again. This left the senior Eisenhower with all the bills of the store.

Jacob took a job at Denison, Texas, and worked until he had paid off the creditors of his former store.

Ike later wrote that, because of this early

experience of his father, he determined never to owe anyone a nickel. The family never used charge accounts. Whenever a purchase was made, the cash must be available.

As is the case in small towns, the people of Abilene knew of Jacob Eisenhower's extraordinary honesty, and he was greatly respected. His father's character greatly influenced Ike in his later life.

Chapter Three

GROWING UP WITH FIVE BROTHERS

There was a good deal of difference in age among the six brothers.

Arthur was the oldest. Ike wrote that he liked to study and was ambitious. Because Ike was four years younger he thought Arthur was very sophisticated, a man about town. Arthur had the best reputation for behavior. He had little interest in tussling with his younger brothers. His parents hardly ever had to discipline him. The athletics so popular with the others did not interest him.

Because of the difference in their ages, the brothers rather paired off according to age. Edgar was two years older than Dwight. They remained close as they grew up. They were both strong and athletic, but Ike was never able to get the better of

1902

Previous pages, Family portrait, David and Ida Eisenhower, rear, standing: Dwight D., Edgar, Earl, Arthur and Roy. Middle front: Milton; above, the electric car at the Eisenhower Museum, Abilene.

Edgar in their many brotherly boxing and wrestling battles. These tussles were not as fierce as fights with outsiders, which were real slugging matches, going on until one or the other was beaten. The two brothers just wrestled around unscientifically, but Ed always came out on top.

In addition to the pain these bouts caused him, Ike was bothered and embarrassed that he could never beat his brother. He determined that sooner or later he would become strong enough to beat his brother when they were equal in size.

After he went to West Point Ike trained hard;

he thought he might win. So he sent Edgar a challenge for any kind of fight the first time they got home together. Edgar accepted the challenge, but they never found a chance to slug it out.

Generally, however, all the brothers faced life as a team. They helped each other through college. In later life each had success in his own field. Friends often asked why there were no black sheep in the family.

Ike felt it was because their parents never quarreled. Although the father and mother rarely showed their emotions, the boys knew that they loved each other. They taught their sons to show concern for others outside the family. Through their example they conveyed many values such as being self-dependent and modestly ambitious.

Ike remembers that his family life was really very happy. He recalled that some accounts called the family "poor." He disagreed, saying that they never thought of themselves as poor and probably were not according to the standards of the times. They always had a good home and good food. They could earn and keep whatever money they could and were permitted to spend all of it as they wished. They worked in stores after school, took summer jobs or raised vegetables and sold them. He could not recall that they ever felt sorry for themselves.

Chapter Four

SCHOLAR, NOT A STUDENT

Dwight Eisenhower did not care very much for the kind of formal education he was given in school. However, he loved to read about the history of Greece and Rome and other ancient nations.

The generals of ancient times became his heroes. Later, he read everything he could find about such great Americans as George Washington. He loved to read about the ancient generals and how they won their battles. The battles of Marathon and Cannae were as real to him as the war games he played with his brothers and friends, real as the day's news. These memories helped him in later life.

He said that of all the ancient generals, Hannibal was his favorite. He chose Hannibal because all that had been written about the ancient general had been written by his enemies, and he always seemed to be an underdog. Ike always had an appreciation for the underdog.

He did not neglect American generals in his reading, and he chose Washington as his hero. He read everything he could find about his battles at Trenton and Princeton, about the terrible hardships at Valley Forge. He admired Washington's patience when the going was rough, the fact that he was strong and self reliant and daring and made sacrifices for others. He was impressed by his character.

Although Ike did not like the formal lessons at school, he probably knew much more about history and the lives of inspiring leaders than the other students, because of the great amount of reading he did with so much enjoyment. Mathematics, science and geography were his favorite formal subjects. These all helped him in many ways in later years.

The young Eisenhower was much more interested in sports and athletics than in studies. The high school did not provide for sports. So the students organized their own games and set up an association to organize athletics. Ike was the association president in his senior year. He took part in almost all the sports.

In his day, few boys finished high school, but Ike was encouraged to continue through. He did not start to shine in school until he studied plane geometry. Almost at once the teacher saw that he was outstanding in figuring out the problems.

After Ike and Edgar graduated from high school, they both worked feverishly to save money. The money was needed so that Ed could enter the University of Michigan. Dwight was determined to have a college education too, but he did not know how this could come about.

Their father always hoped that all his family could have a good education. That ambition was realized by four of them.

When Edgar went to college, all his younger brothers pitched in and worked and sent him what help they could. But he worked at the university and managed to pay most of his own way. Ed, in turn, provided financing for Earl's education at the University of Washington. Versatile Milton played in a dance band, corrected English papers and wrote magazine articles to finance his education at Kansas State University. As vice-consul at Edinburgh, Scotland, Milton did graduate work at the University there.

Ike's educational experiences were entirely different.

After Ike had been out of high school and working for two years, a friend, Everett "Swede" Hazlett, suggested that Ike might be able to get an appointment to one of the U.S. military academies. This would be either West Point for the army or Annapolis for the navy. While Ike worked nights

Ike loved to play baseball. Here he is shown, second from the right in the top row, with his high school team.

as a fireman at the Abilene ice house, he and Swede studied together daytimes.

Ike passed the examination for West Point and received the appointment. This meant that his advanced education would be given to him at government expense. He received this appointment over hundreds of other hopeful applicants from his area. He felt that his father's reputation influenced Senator Joseph Bristow and the others who recommended him for the appointment.

Chapter Five

FROM PRAIRIE TO A HIGH POINT

Dwight David Eisenhower arrived at the United States Military Academy at West Point, New York, on June 14, 1911. He was sworn in that night as a cadet. Remembering that night, he wrote later, "Suddenly the flag itself meant something....Across half a century I can look back and see a rawboned, gawky Kansas boy from the farm country, earnestly repeating the words that would make him a cadet."

By the end of the next day, however, life at the academy had brought Ike back down to earth. It was traditional at West Point for the Plebes to be harrassed by upperclassmen. Since the Plebes felt important, they resented this treatment. Their older fellows shouted at them from morning until night. They were never allowed just to hurry but were made to do everthing in double quick time. Every little item, such as picking up clothes, bringing in bedding, and keeping shoulders back provoked shouted orders. However, Ike decided that much of this was done so that they would have little time to think about their troubles and to become homesick. There was no time to think.

Despite such common complaints, Ike had little difficulty adjusting to the rigid life of the Academy. One small problem was that he could not keep step to military music. To overcome his rhythmic problems, he had to spend some time in the awkward squad. Finally he learned to coordinate his feet with the drum beat.

Another embarrassing moment came when he saluted a drum major, thinking he was an officer.

His main reason for wanting a higher education was to take part in athletics. He was too small for the Academy football team, but he was good at baseball. However, he worked hard; by the football season of 1912, he was heavy enough and good enough to play regularly on the varsity team.

Then he was injured in a game. Shortly after that, he was thrown from a horse, further injuring his knee. From that time on, to his sad disappointment, he was not able to play in rough sports. In fact, his knee continued to bother him severely for the rest of his life.

School discipline bothered Ike. He said himself he was not a good cadet. Early on, he was in

Ike's West Point graduation picture shows a confident young man who managed to overcome an inability to march in step, and who, more importantly, overcame his tendency to earn demerits in discipline and who graduated as a fine scholar. His greatest regret was the injury which kept him from a promising West Point athletic career.

the lowest quarter of his class in discipline.

Ike loved to play jokes on the upperclassmen. One day, for example, an upperclassman named Adler found Ike and a friend guilty of some small infraction of regulations. He ordered them to report to his room after tattoo in "full-dress coats." This was supposed to mean complete uniform.

However, the two cadets decided they would obey the order literally and wear nothing but the heavy coats. When the time for the appointment came, they put on their full-dress coats as ordered, but were otherwise completely naked. They marched into Adler's room and solemnly told him that Cadets Eisenhower and Atkins reported as ordered.

The corporal made them suffer a good deal for this prank.

However, as Ike pointed out, in spite of his many demerits for small matters of discipline, "...my West Point record was not all bad....One report on my early performance even said...that I was 'born to command.' "

Because of his leg injury, Ike was not even certain that he would get a second lieutenant's commission as his classmates would when they graduated. At that time he was not even particularly interested in an army career. However, after graduation he did get his commission. This marked the beginning of one of the most brilliant careers in the history of the U.S. armed forces.

It is strange to think that many critics have

said that Eisenhower was not well enough educated for the high posts he received. During his entire lifetime, he read books on the widest variety of learned subjects.

His graduation from West Point was only one step in a unique educational career. His formal education extended through portions of almost thirty years.

Dwight Eisenhower graduated as first in his class from the Command and General Staff College at Fort Leavenworth. He also graduated first in his class from the Army War College at Fort McNair. This was one of the highest educational honors available to an army man. This educational distinction was the ambition of almost every army officer.

It probably could be said that Ike was the most educated man ever to become President of the United States.

He even graduated from army Cooks and Bakers School.

In addition to his formal schooling, he had a most unusual memory. It was said that he remembered every memo that he had written and every conversation that had taken place in his long career.

Chapter Six

FROM POST TO POST

Ike's first army assignment was at Fort Sam Houston, San Antonio, Texas. Because of trouble with Mexico along the border, the army had been strengthening its forces in the area.

There Ike met Mamie Geneva Doud. Soon they were going out almost every night when Ike was not on duty. He was still paying off his old debts. So they often went to the Original Restaurant, along the picturesque banks of the San Antonio River. There they could get a good dinner for two for as little as a dollar, including tip.

The young lieutenants at the fort did not take army life too seriously. One evening Ike was with a group of other lieutenants and bet one of them five dollars he could climb up a metal brace holding a flagpole, using only his hands. He threw off his shirt and was almost at the top, when he heard a voice bellowing from below. It was the commanding officer of the post. He was told to get down immediately and put on his shirt. The commandant raked him over the coals and departed with the cool command that there had better not be a repetition on anyone's part. Ike was more worried about the bet than about the Colonel. However, it was agreed that there would not be a payoff. He got his five dollars back.

Ike and Mamie Doud became engaged. He had an opportunity to go into the Air Force. When Mamie's family objected, he gave up on the idea.

This decision seemed to change him from his carefree ways. The decision made Ike begin to think about his responsibility to perform every duty to the best of his ability so that his army record would be good. This would be true of every duty, whether he liked it or not.

Ike and Mamie were married in Denver and spent a brief honeymoon at Colorado Springs. Then they had eight hours with his parents at Abilene and returned to the post. There Ike reported that Mamie was "...young, full of life, and attractive, was the pet of the post."

To keep her safe, Ike gave Mamie a pistol and showed her how to use it. One morning Ike suggested they pretend someone was breaking in. Ike reported that the pistol was hidden so well behind a bedding roll that it probably would have taken her

Lieutenant and Mamie Doud Eisenhower in their wedding portrait, Denver Colorado, July 1, 1916.

"a week" to get it out and confront a burglar. He would just have to keep on with his assignment to make camp safer.

By this time, the U.S. was preparing for World War I. Ike had several assignments to train officers and men for fighting in Europe. Then he was sent to Camp Meade, Maryland. Meanwhile, the Eisenhowers had their first son, Doud Dwight, nicknamed Icky.

The new assignment was to organize a tank corps for overseas duty. At this time, tanks were so new in warfare that little was known about them. They were not being built fast enough to fill the need. Nevertheless, Ike managed to get a regiment ready. He was deeply disappointed because he was not permitted to go overseas to command the unit. Instead, he was sent to build a new camp at Gettysburg, Pennsylvania.

At Gettysburg, Ike proved to have great skills in organization and in finding new ways of doing things. These included starting a telegraphic school and a motor school. All these experiences were preparing him for greater things ahead.

Chapter Seven

TANKS AND TRAGEDY

Ike helped to organize the return of the World War I army from Europe. He went on to many other assignments after the war.

One of the most interesting of these was taking a group of army trucks in a convoy across the United States. Strange as it seems, this had never been done. Some thought it was impossible because of the condition of the roads across the country. Ike learned a great deal about the countryside and the many towns and people they passed on the long and tiresome way.

In California the roads were the best they had found anywhere in the country, but even there they averaged only ten miles per hour. There were broken fan belts, broken spark plugs, constant problems with brakes, motorcycles that gave out at almost every turn, along with every other problem that ever hit a motor vehicle.

At the end of the trip, the Governor of California, William D. Stephens, compared them to the immortal Forty-Niners, the pioneer gold miners who rushed to California. They were paraded through the streets of Sacramento as heroes, and fireworks displays lit up the night sky. It is hard to imagine today such a fanfare for crossing the country by car.

It is interesting to note that one of the things Ike learned was the importance of good highways. He remembered that the reports of every officer on the journey called for greater efforts to be made to stir interest in better roads. When he was president, Ike recalled the truck trip. He also remembered the wonderful superhighways called Autobahns he had seen in Germany. When he became president, he decided to promote such road building in the U.S. He was responsible for the great Interstate Highway system which now blankets most of the country.

In a way, people in cars crossing the country in a few days on Interstate 80, or those using other interstates, can thank that early truck convoy for the magnificent road system in use today.

Back at Camp Meade, Ike became reacquainted with an old friend, Colonel George Patton. Patton had been a pioneer in the use of tanks during the First World War. Ike and Patton began to experiment in new methods of tank warfare.

During World War I tanks had been used

mainly to go ahead of foot soldiers, destroying machine gun nests. They did not need to go faster than about three miles per hour. This was the speed at which infantry could advance. The tanks had to be built heavy and strong enough to withstand machine gun and anti-tank guns.

Ike and Patton opposed the slow, lumbering tanks. They believed that tanks should be speedy, should attack in mass, break into the enemy's defensive positions and cause confusion. This might make it possible to surround and capture an enemy quickly. This was an entirely new philosophy of warfare.

They believed that modern warfare required speed and firepower and reliable operation and that tank armor should withstand considerable firepower but remain mobile.

In one of their experiments with a new tank, they took it completely apart, including the engine, until not a bolt or nut was connected. They were not sure they could put it back in running order. However, they did manage to put it back together, and it ran smoothly.

Despite their great progress, the army was still not convinced that tanks could be of much use. Nevertheless, the early teamwork of Eisenhower and Patton was preparing them both for a war that was to come.

Ike loved to play poker. With his great memory he could recall every play. He seldom lost. He

Military Hall in the Eisenhower Museum at Abilene. Ike was one of the major figures in preparing the army for the motor age. He worked with tanks and artillery with Patton and others, pioneered in overland transport and helped the nation realize the importance of good roads. The Military Hall at the Eisenhower Presidential Library has many items of ordnance and equipment which help to demonstrate Ike's interest and ability in that area.

became known as one of the best players in the army. He often won enough to help him out of his money problems.

Then in one game at Camp Meade a young officer lost far more than he could afford. The other players learned of this and let him win the money back. This lesson was not lost on Ike. He decided that he would never take such advantage of a person again. He quit poker playing.

At Camp Meade, Ike coached the football team quite successfully. He had coached army teams off and on for much of his early career.

During the stay at Camp Meade, the Eisenhowers finally paid off their last debts. They decided they could afford some of life's comforts. They hired a local girl as a maid. They did not know she had just recovered from scarlet fever.

Unfortunately, the girl gave young Icky the disease. Ike reported that they made every possible effort to save his life, bringing in top specialists from the Johns Hopkins Medical school in nearby Baltimore.

Ike was not permitted to be with the little boy in his room. He had to sit on a porch outside where he could look in and wave and talk to him. He hardly left the hospital. Those were the days when little could be done outside of hope and prayer, as contrasted with current times when scarlet fever has been conquered by modern medicine. The year's end brought the tragedy of the loss of their firstborn son. Ike called this the one greatest tragedies of his life, one which he was never able to forget.

Chapter Eight

LIFE IN PANAMA

In early 1922, Ike was transferred to Panama.

He and Mamie settled down in an isolated post called Camp Gaillard. The roofs leaked; bats came in; insects swarmed; the weather was frightfully hot and humid, but they managed to keep up their spirits and enjoy the limited social life of the base.

One of the major problems of the canal at that location was the continuing landslides. Every so often huge quantities of soil would slide down and block the canal. Then great dredges would arrive to dig it all out again. The excitement of these slides helped to break the monotony of being isolated so far from most activities.

Years later Ike was flying over that part of

the canal when he noticed with horror that the place where they once lived had also slid into the canal and had been removed.

In Panama Ike's commanding officer was General Fox Conner. He was very fond of the Eisenhowers, and they greatly appreciated his friendship. The general had a large library. When he discovered that Ike had little interest in military history he urged the young officer to study the accounts of military action. This he felt would help him in his career. For nearly three years, the general guided Ike through the military tactics of many wars: "...sort of a graduate school in military affairs and the humanities," as Ike put it. He became so intrigued with military history that he read some of the books as many as three times.

Most places in the area could only be reached by horseback, so Ike had to choose an army horse. He had to make his selection of his personal horse from among twenty that were left after several officers had already had their choice. None of the remaining horses had been trained.

Ike asked one of the soldiers on duty to help him select a mount. Sergeant Lopez' knowledge of horses and his personality impressed Ike so much that before he chose a horse he asked the sergeant to be his orderly.

Then Ike chose a large deep black gelding, standing taller than sixteen hands. Ike was an authority, and he declared the horse was splendidly built in his hindquarters. However, in his forward part he was more like a mule. His head was large and perched on a short thick neck. Ike guessed he could be stubborn. Since Ike had ridden, trained and cared for horses beginning at an early age, he decided that this was the best horse available for jungle use. Lopez was pleased. Lopez chose a horse for himself, and the little group of Ike and Lopez and the two horses almost immediately became a close foursome.

Ike's horse was named Blackie. Blackie trained easily. He learned to obey every command made by Ike, to trot and canter and to learn a complete set of tricks.

Blackie's obedience once saved his life. On one trip into the highlands, Blackie became mired in quicksand. As he struggled to free himself, he sank deeper and deeper into the mire. Then Ike called out, "Blackie, halt!" Immediately the horse became still and stopped sinking until his master and others could pull him out.

Because of his obedience, intelligence and ability to do tricks, Ike said Blackie's reputation soared at the post.

One of his tricks was to walk up and down stairs. Most horses refuse to do this.

Blackie's appearance at a Canal horse show was a favorite memory of Ike's. He recalled how Blackie responded to the crowd and climbed some steps like a ham actor. Ike made him get down on his front knees as if bowing. He tilted his ears forward and looked like a champion.

Ike's experiences in training animals and men made him always aware of the real worth of every individual.

Mamie went to Denver for the birth of their new son, John. She and the baby later returned to Panama for the rest of their stay in the Canal Zone.

Chapter Nine

MORE EXPERIENCE, MORE EDUCATION

Back in the states, the Eisenhowers were sent to several posts, including study for Ike at the Command and General Staff School and the War College.

Another duty was to write the guidebook to World War I battle monuments. This took him through much of France. There he had a chance to get acquainted with the French people and to know the countryside.

Work on the guidebook also brought him into contact with General John G. Pershing. General Pershing had been the commander of all overseas American military forces in World War I. Ike helped the general in writing his memoirs.

Ike recalled that the general was always late as much as an hour for every meeting. Ike had a difficult time, and he was greatly embarrassed when he had to make apologies to the host, but time apparently meant nothing to General Pershing. He never made excuses for keeping everyone waiting.

The next assignment was at the office of the Assistant Secretary of War. Ike was part of a team which studied how the country could tool up for a future world war. They visited factories to see how the manufacturing processes could be changed over to make wartime supplies. They interviewed such experts as Bernard Baruch. Mr. Baruch had headed the World War I War Industries Board.

For Ike, this was an important part of learning how American industry could be converted to make the guns and ships and supplies needed in war time.

The next step was to become an aide to General Douglas MacArthur. They worked closely together in Washington. "Working with him brought a new dimension to my experience," Ike wrote.

Chapter Ten

ON TO THE PHILIPPINES!

General MacArthur's father had been the last American military governor in the Philippines. The U.S. had controlled the Philippines since the War with Spain. Now America was giving the people of the Philippines their freedom. They were to have their own government and armed forces.

General Douglas MacArthur was sent to the Philippines as military adviser to the new Philippine government. Everything had to be started from scratch. Ike had become such a help to the general in Washington that he was assigned to work with MacArthur to build the Philippine military forces.

Even before they left Washington, Ike had worked out a defense program for the Philippines.

The main problem was finding the money for that kind of program in such a poor nation. They had to keep cutting their plans for lack of money.

Mamie and John stayed in Washington so that John could finish the eighth grade of school.

Ike and his staff set up 90 small military stations across the Philippines, on the various islands. They bought a few surplus U.S. planes to fly back and forth among the stations. Ike learned to fly and did some pioneer aviation work in the Philippines.

Ike and President Manuel Quezon of the Philippines became good friends. The president and Ike often talked about taxes, education, honesty in government and other subjects, as well as defense.

Ike's family came to the Philippines, and John went to school in the mountains at Baguio.

Ike reported that most of the Philippine people favored Hitler, but they gave very little thought to Japan as a war threat.

When World War II broke out in Europe in 1939, Ike asked to be returned to Washington. He felt sure that the U.S. would be forced into the war in Europe. He wanted to help prepare for that war. Both MacArthur and President Quezon urged him to stay. However, he was "...determined to do everything I could to make sure I would not miss this crisis of our country....For me, the next six years would be thronged with challenges and chances, work and decisions."

Ike was not immediately assigned to Washington. Instead he was sent to a regiment in Fort Lewis, Washington. In this region, far from Washington headquarters, he had little hope of ever becoming an army general. Nevertheless, he said he would always do the best he could.

The approaching war changed all this. Ike helped as thousands of draftees came to Fort Lewis. Then he led troops on exercises in Louisiana.

After the Japanese attack at Pearl Harbor, the fate of the Philippines was on the mind of everyone. Ike probably knew more about the defense of the islands than anyone else in the country. He had prepared lengthy memos on the best way to defend the islands from attack. He guessed this was the reason for his next assignment, when a sudden call brought him to Washington for emergency duty.

Ike joined the staff of General George C. Marshall, who led the war operations. Before long he became Chief of Operations and was promoted to Major General. Action in the Philippines was not to be a part of his life.

Chapter Eleven

ON TO EUROPE! ON TO AFRICA!

Almost as suddenly as he had come to Washington, Ike was sent by General Marshall to London to command American European operations. By this time, most of Europe had already been captured by Adolf Hitler's Nazi army.

Most of the countries of North Africa that had been under French rule had also fallen into the hands of the Axis powers—Italy and Germany. The U.S. and its Allies decided the first comeback against Hitler would be in North Africa. American and British troops would do most of the fighting.

Ike was chosen to command the entire operation. It was known as Operation Torch. Ike's principal assistant was General George Patton.

British General Bernard L. Montgomery led

the drive across Africa from the east. the Axis forces were under German Field Marshall Erwin Rommel. He was known as the Desert Fox because he understood the ways of fighting in the desert. American and British forces landed first at Morocco then at Algiers, Oran and Casablanca. This placed Rommel between the two Allies.

Men and tanks moved back and forth in the terrible desert heat, suffering and dying on both sides.

The Allies suffered a temporary setback at Kasserine Pass, but went on to destroy all Axis resistance in North Africa.

More than 250,000 of them surrendered. The war in North Africa was over on May 12, 1942. During the campaign in Africa, Ike had crisscrossed the region personally, visiting the war fronts. He had many close calls.

On one of his flights, he used an old plane and barely made it over the Atlas Mountains. When Ike ordered the plane repaired for the return trip, the repair crew told him it could never fly again and would have to be scrapped. If the plane had crashed, world history could have been changed.

Hitler's main Axis partner, Italy, lay just across from North Africa. The island of Sicily came first. In July Ike commanded the invasion of Sicily. In September his forces landed at Salerno on the Italian mainland. Then the Allied forces moved up the peninsula of Italy.

"Although they did not reach Rome before winter," according to the *Journal of Military History,* "Ike had managed to drive the Axis from the Mediterranean. In the process he had welded together a team of British and American officers unequaled in the annals of warfare for its cooperation."

Because of this record, even while fierce and bloody fighting was going on in Italy under his command, Ike was given an even greater responsibility.

General Dwight David Eisenhower was chosen to be the Supreme Commander of all Allied forces in Europe. He was to take charge of the campaign to invade Europe and overcome Hitler. This campaign was given the code name Operation Overlord.

In only a few months Ike had risen from an almost unknown American Lieutenant Colonel to the highest command post in modern military history.

The invasion of Sicily marked the beginning of the Allies' long hard drive to win Europe back from Hitler and Mussolini. Here the semi-invalid President Franklin D. Roosevelt is shown after he made the long trip to Sicily to confer with Eisenhower.

Chapter Twelve

"CRUSADE IN EUROPE"

Preparing for Operation Overlord, Ike returned to the U.S. to confer with American leaders. He had a conference with President Franklin D. Roosevelt. Roosevelt was in bed with the flu, and they talked in his bedroom. They discussed the future of Europe after the war. If the Russians succeeded in coming into Germany from the East, how much of Europe would they occupy? How would the western Allies arrange matters with the Russians?

Ike did not trust the Russians. Time and again he had written that they did not keep their word. Later he wrote that his experiences since 1941 had convinced him that the Soviet Union would sooner or later turn against the United States and would become a potential enemy.

Ike knew that most of the British leaders also were more trusting of the Russians than he was. Roosevelt insisted that the Soviet leaders could be depended upon. The president said he had already made up his mind about dividing up Europe with Russia, and the matter was closed. The Russians were to be allowed to penetrate Germany to a certain point without interference from the Allies. There was nothing Ike could do.

This had been a very difficult decision for the U.S. and its allies. Without the help of the Russians coming in from the East, the Allies were not strong enough to beat the Germans.

If the Allies did not have some kind of an agreement with the Russians, the Soviet armies might sweep across most of Europe while the Allied armies were bogged down on the western front. And so Roosevelt, Stalin and Churchill had agreed on the division of Europe into East and West. This was done in spite of the fact that dictatorial Russian control in eastern Europe might overwhelm freedom in all the East European countries.

Returning to London, Ike was caught in the worst London fog he had ever seen. His aides had to walk in front of the car to lead the way. They had a difficult time even finding the front door of the commander's new office. Ike hoped that this was not a sign that they would have to feel their way entirely across Europe.

Ike held weekly meetings with British Prime Minister Winston Churchill. Churchill worried that an invasion of Europe would bring about terrible loss of American and British lives. He felt the Allies might lose as many as 90 percent of the

Few men in history have had the opportunity to work with and to get to know so many famous historical personalities. Here Ike confers with the legendary Winston Churchill, wartime Prime Minister of Great Britain.

attacking men, but he went along with the invasion plans.

At one time Ike told Churchill about a bet he had made with General Montgomery. Ike bet they would end the war in Europe by the end of 1944, and he still believed that.

Among the many meetings in preparing for the attack one conference assembled possibly the most important group of people ever gathered under a single roof, Ike wrote. The King and Prime Minister of England and all the major commanders were present. Their plans were being carried out on an enormous scale. Never before had so much war materiel and so many men been gathered for an attack on a single area—all of this to be ferried across the treacherous English Channel. According to Ike this was completely unprecedented in military history.

Timing of the attack was very important. If it were to succeed, Hitler's forces would have to be taken by surprise. The location of the landing would have to be the most important surprise.

Getting the enormous invading forces across the English Channel was one of the most difficult parts of the whole operation.

As the time approached, the weather was bad. The crossings and landings could not be successful in bad weather.

The decision was described in the *Journal of Military History*: "D-Day? or delay?

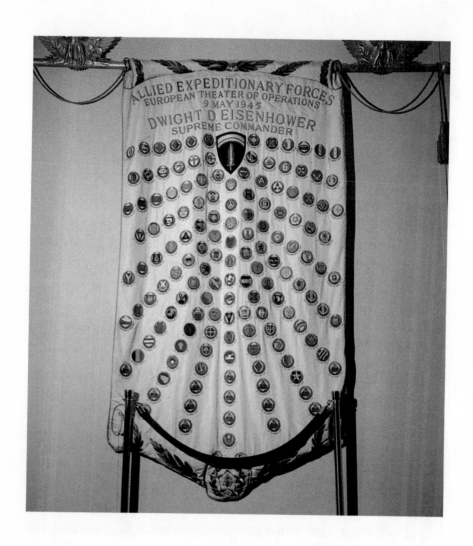

"Allied Expeditionary Forces, European Theater of Operations, 9 May, 1945, Dwight D. Eisenhower, Supreme Commander." The Eisenhower museum at Abilene proudly displays the banner showing the symbols of the great force commanded by Ike during World War II.

"It was June 6, 1944, three-thirty a.m. and, rain was pounding down so hard, the generals had to shout to be heard over the noise.

"Out in the English Channel 5,000 ships were waiting for the word to head for the beaches of Normandy.

"His advisors were split.

"Ike said 'Go!'" And oh how they went!

The attack on the beaches of Normandy in France was of a size and fury never equalled before or since. Of course, it did succeed; the Germans were driven from Paris; the Allied forces sliced across the continent.

Ike always praised the gallantry of the men who had to carry out in actual combat the strategy prepared by his high command. He admired the tremendous courage they showed.

One of the luckiest breaks of the war came at the town of Remagen on the Rhine River. The Germans failed to destroy the great bridge at Remagen. The American army captured this critical bridge. Without the bridge the crossing of the Rhine would have been much more difficult and time-consuming.

By April 1, 1945, the Allies were ready for a three-pronged attack into Germany on the western front. On April 11, U.S. forces reached the Elbe River, and General George Patton's third army approached the border of Czechoslovakia. Ike ordered the Allied forces to halt. This permitted the

Russians to march into Berlin and force the city to surrender. Later, to General Patton's dismay, the Russians occupied Prague, the capital of Czechoslovakia, while the Americans were ordered to wait outside. This was all according to the arrangements made by Stalin, Roosevelt and Churchill.

However, many critics say that Ike should have disregarded his orders, that he should have moved forward to take Berlin and Czechoslovakia and as much else of eastern Europe as could be captured before the Russians could get there.

This argument has never been resolved and probably never will be. The result of holding back the Allied force, of course, was to place all of eastern Europe in Communist control, and the free world has been in turmoil ever since.

Of course, the American forces did meet with the Russians after the Soviet forces had captured Berlin, and there were great celebrations as the war came to an official end with the German surrender to the Allies on May 7, 1945.

On that day Ike sent word to General Omar Bradley to be sure that all firing stopped at midnight of the eighth. The war with Hitler in Europe was over. Ike described his tremendous relief that he no longer had to make such tremendous life and death decisions.

C C/S.

The mission of this Allied Force was fulfilled at 3.00 a.m., local time, May 7, 1945. Eisenhower.

To C C/S.

A detailed report on signing of armistice and my recommendations respecting government announcement follow immediately. I believe earliest although hostilities do not officially cease until one minute after midnight in night of May 8/9, I believe, as explained in longer telegram to follow that announcement should be at earliest hour that coordination can be achieved. Eisenhower

The famous letter from Dwight D. Eisenhower, announcing the end of World War II, is reproduced here.

63

Chapter Thirteen

HONORS

The war had been ended sooner than most people had hoped. Ike had led the greatest army in world history to the greatest of all victories. He had become one of the world's most celebrated military heroes.

As the victorious Supreme Commander, Ike received, perhaps, more honors than had ever before been given to a conquering general.

Among the most important of those honors, he received the British Order of Merit, considered the finest honor Britain can give, and also the British Order of the Bath.

On another occasion, he was taken in a carriage into the old City of London to be made a Freeman of the City of London at the ancient Guildhall there. Afterward Ike and Winston

Among the many mementoes of Ike at the Eisenhower museum in Abilene is this panel which holds some of the many distinguished medals won by the general during his long career.

Churchill stood on a balcony greeting a crowd which was so large that every inch of pavement in the square below them seemed to be covered with people.

When Ike returned to the U.S. he could hardly believe the crowds that came out to greet him on the streets with such wild enthusiasm. His cavalcades traveled for hours past sidewalks thronged with people covering every available vantage point and hanging out the windows.

His home town of Abilene honored him with a three-mile-long homecoming parade.

Note: The speech made by Ike at the Guildhall was reprinted in full in the New York Times. Because it has been called one of the notable addresses of modern times, it has been reprinted in full beginning on page 100.

Chapter Fourteen

AFTERMATH

As one of the Allied leaders in Germany, Ike met regularly with Marshall G. K. Zhukov, the Soviet Representative. They became quite friendly, but Ike could never get Zhukov to understand the ways of a democracy. At one time an American newspaper said that the Marshall was shorter than his wife and that they had three children. Zhukov said this was untrue. He demanded that the newspaper be punished.

Ike explained that one of the reasons he was a soldier was because he wanted to assure free speech and a free press. But the Marshall insisted that if Ike had been described improperly in a publication in his country he would see to it that the newspaper was put out of business.

Getting the American troops back to the U.S.

was one of Ike's most difficult jobs. Of course, everyone wanted to get back at once, and this was impossible. However, the task was finally accomplished.

Back in the U.S. Ike became Army Chief of Staff. When this duty was over, he kept three secretaries and numerous researchers and editors busy writing his best-selling book *Crusade in Europe.*

Next, Ike took over as President of Columbia University in New York City. He followed Nicholas Murray Butler, who had been the university president for almost fifty years.

While in this post Ike made many changes to bring the university up-to-date. He also enthusiastically took up the hobby of painting.

One of Ike's accomplishments at Columbia was to get the various departments to work more closely together. He established several important new projects, such as The American Assembly, a new engineering center, the Citizenship Education Project, the Conservation of Human Resources program and the Institute for the Study of War and Peace.

While at Columbia, Ike and Mamie bought an old farmhouse near the battlefield at Gettysburg, Pennsylvania. This was to be their home in future years, and they gave much attention to fixing it up.

For Ike's next assignment, he took a leave of absence from Columbia. He took over as first commander of the North Atlantic Treaty Organization

As a prelude to the larger presidency, Dwight D. Eisenhower became President of Columbia University. Here he is shown leading one of the academic processions at the University.

(NATO). This organization was designed to protect all the twelve European member nations from attack. He spent months visiting with the heads of the various nations and their military advisers.

As NATO commander, Ike devoted much of his time to encouraging all the participating nations to work together. If they did so "...the security of western Europe would be assured. The region would then become...as powerful as any other in the world." He also urged the nations of Europe to join together in some form of a government of Europe.

Previous pages, while he was president at Columbia University, Ike and Mamie began to prepare for his retirement by buying this home at Gettysburg, Pennsylvania, and they spent much time restoring the pleasant homestead. Ike thought it odd that he should own property in the area where some of his forebears had lived.

Chapter Fifteen

MR. PRESIDENT

Almost as soon as World War II ended, politicians of both Republican and Democratic parties had begun urging Ike to run for President. Finally he agreed, but still without much enthusiasm. At one time he told Emmet Hughes that it didn't matter very much if the politicians did not select him. He said he had a lot of fishing to catch up with.

Of course, he did become president. During his first term he had serious health problems. His son John and brother Milton felt he should not run for a second term, but Mamie did not object. She felt that Ike would be happier trying to finish what he had started in his first term.

In the election race with Adlai Stevenson, he was even more successful in the second race than in the first. He entered his second term as president with great popular support.

The Eisenhower inaugural at Washington, D.C., January 21, 1953, brought together several generations of famous American statesmen, some of whom are shown in this famous photograph, including Herbert Hoover, Harry S. Truman, Eisenhower and Richard Nixon.

74

During his terms as president, Ike was called a "do-nothing" president. On the contrary, today more recent historians have begun to realize how much he accomplished. Even some of those who criticized him the most began to praise his work as president. One of these later spoke enthusiastically of how Ike tried to cut down the power of military leaders—how he warned against atomic war.

Others referred approvingly to his speech when he said, "We are in an armaments race. Where will it lead us? At worst, to atomic warfare. At best, to robbing every people and nation on earth of the fruits of their own toil."

His friends pointed out that this "do-nothing" president had created a network of air bases to surround the Soviet Union. They said he had worked to form treaties to contain Communism. He called for freedom of the Russian satellite nations in eastern Europe. He "averted a broader conflict in Vietnam."

During Ike's presidency the nation was prosperous and at peace. Inflation and taxes were cut. The St. Lawrence Seaway was opened. Ten million people were added to Social Security. He prohibited racial discrimination in government positions. The first civil rights act in 57 years came about during his administration. He sent federal troops to Little Rock, Arkansas, to enforce the court order to integrate schools there.

All of his accomplishments came about while

After his second victory over Adlai Stevenson, Eisenhower was inaugurated for his second term on January 21, 1957. He paused with his vice president to view the inaugural parade.

Viewing the inaugural parade are Eisenhower, his grandchildren, Barbara Ann and David, with Vice-President Richard Nixon and his children, Julie and Tricia.

the opposite party controlled both houses of Congress.

Ike had a lifelong experience in finding the right people to work with him. Richard Rhodes wrote that he was the "most skillful delegator of authority the nation has known." Things seemed to run smoothly while he appeared to sit back and do nothing. This is supposed to be one of the marks of a top leader.

Many historians now say that he was much more responsible for his decisions than was thought possible at the time.

Many claimed Ike was a "prisoner" of Secretary of State John Foster Dulles. However, Ike said "Dulles made no move without consulting me." Ike accepted the final responsibility for decisions. He said that on a great number of occasions he made decisions which were the opposite of those advising him.

Mamie enjoyed some of the life of the White House. However, she wrote that she had to struggle all the time with the personal budget and had a hard time making ends meet, because the president must pay for all of his personal expenses. The government only pays for the official entertaining of the president.

Opposite, On his famous visit to America, Russian leader Nikita Khrushchev met President Eisenhower at Camp David, Maryland, September 25, 1959.

President and Mrs. Eisenhower welcome Queen Elizabeth and Prince Philip to the White House, October 12, 1957.

Chapter Sixteen

RETIRED

The day the Eisenhowers left the White House they moved into their beloved house at Gettysburg. Mamie wrote that the first five years of retirement formed "...one of the most enjoyable periods of our entire life." At last, Ike had more time for his painting, his beloved golf and the reading he enjoyed so much.

About painting he wrote that he longed for more hours of daylight for his painting. In order to combine exercise with his painting he commented humorously that he might install a painting outfit on his golf cart.

Their Gettysburg farm was not far from Elizabethville in Pennsylvania's Lykens Valley where Ike's grandfather Jacob Eisenhower had bought a farm. Ike thought it was strange that so much later

In retirement, for the first time Ike could enjoy the leisure activities which he liked so much and for which he seldom before had time. Here he proudly exhibits his success on a fishing trip at West Greenwich, Rhode Island, September 19, 1958.

he had managed at last to "return to his roots."

An important event in Ike's retirement was the dedication of the Dwight D. Eisenhower Library on May 2, 1962. This is one of the National Archives and Records Service system of Presidential Libraries. But it is unique among these libraries. It is not just a library and museum housed in a single building. Rather it is a collection of five buildings known as the Eisenhower Center.

There is the Eisenhower Family Home, on its original site and with its original furnishings; the museum; the library building; the Visitors Center, and the Place of Meditation. The latter was intended as a chapel and burial site for the Eisenhower family.

The body of three-year-old Doud Dwight Eisenhower was moved there and interred in the building.

The other Eisenhower memorial, at Denison, Texas, has an interesting history. Apparently Ike did not know where he was born. On his West Point application he listed his birthplace as Tyler, Texas. He was the only one of the Eisenhower brothers to be born in Texas. The others were all born in Kansas.

After Ike became prominent, a Denison elementary school principal, Jennie Jackson, remembered a David Eisenhower as a baby in Denison. She wrote to the general; he could not recall and suggested that she write his mother. His mother

For my friend
Howard Young.   Dwight D. Eisenhower

replied that, of course, Dwight David was born in Denison, in a two-story house on the corner of Lamar and Day streets.

As a result of Jennie Jackson's interest, a group purchased the home and deeded it to the city of Denison. The restored house and surrounding property were then deeded to the state in 1958. The memorial is now called the Eisenhower Birthplace State Historic Site.

During his retirement Ike continued his writing. He is now considered to have been a very skillful writer. His work included his *Mandate for Peace* and *Waging of Peace.* In his writing he explained much about his philosophy of government. That is, he knew what government could do for the people. He did everything he could to make certain that government really was serving the people.

Eisenhower had led the greatest forces of war in world history. However, he hated war and called it stupid, tragic, the worst of all human activities. He said the world is unbelieveably damaged by the creative people lost to war.

In both war and politics, Ike was "middle of the road." He declared that those who stick to the center must have more courage because they are

Opposite, Ike became surprisingly good at one of his hobbies. He loved to paint. Reproduced here is his picture of a waterfall.

attacked from both sides. He was one of the few leaders courageous enough to speak out against despotism on both the left and the right.

Mamie wrote that the basis of his strength was his "...unfailing belief in and love of his country."

That country paid final tribute to its hero following his death on March 28, 1969. On April 2, 1969, the grounds of the Presidential Library at Abilene were overflowing with people who had come to attend the funeral of the late president. Newspaper reporters and television cameras from all over the world were present as the body of Dwight David Eisenhower was laid to rest in the Place of Meditation. Upon her death, Mrs. Eisenhower was also buried there.

Summarizing Dwight David Eisenhower's life, the *Reader's Digest* declared: "For most of his life, what he thought he really wanted to do was to be a cowboy in Argentina. Instead, he organized an army and ran a war and guided the strongest nation in the world for eight hard years....He didn't give a damn about discipline, but he learned not only to live by its rules himself but also to confer its lifesaving strength on whole armies. He didn't give a damn about offices and position and rank, but he

Previous pages, Ike and Mamie visit the library of the Eisenhower center at Abilene, Kansas. Following page, The Place of Meditation at the center, where the Eisenhowers are buried.

took them all on because he believed he could handle them better than anyone else available."

The *Dictionary of Military Biography* also summarized his life: "Although never a battlefield commander, Ike was nevertheless a great general, perhaps the best of his century....He had, as MacArthur once said and Churchill repeated, the gift of being able to see the whole problem.

"Eisenhower was never a war president. Indeed, his proudest boast was that for eight years he kept the peace; his next boast was that he balanced the budget. His critics called him a do-nothing president, but by the end of the 1960's many of those critics would like to have seen Ike back in office."

Today, hundreds of thousands of visitors flock to the Eisenhower Center in Abilene, Kansas, to pay tribute to the great General and President. There in his library and museum are the millions of letters and other items that will help future generations understand his life.

The Eisenhower library at the memorial center contains a huge collection of materials concerning the life and work of the late General of the Army and President of the United States.

HIGHLIGHTS

1890, October 14, born at Denison, Texas

1909, May 23, high school graduation

1911, June 11, enters West Point, army military academy

1915, June 12, graduates from West point

1915, June, first army assignment at Fort Sam Houston, Texas

1916, marries Mamie Geneva Doud

1918, October 14, promoted to Lieutenant Colonel

1920, July 2, reverted to peacetime rank of Major

1922-1924, stationed in Canal Zone

1926, June, 18, graduated from Command and General Staff School, Ft. Leavenworth, Kansas, first in class of 245

1926, August, battalion commander, 24th Infantry, Ft. Benning, Georgia

1927, January, completed service on American Battle Monuments Commission

1928, June 30, graduated from Army War college

1929, November, joins staff of Assistant Secretary of War

While Dwight D. Eisenhower was growing up in this modest but comfortable home in Abilene, Kansas, who could have imagined that he would become one of the most famous figures in world history?

1933, February, chief military aide to Army Chief of Staff General Douglas MacArthur

1935, September, assigned to MacArthur as military adviser to the Philippine government

1936, July 1, promoted to lieutenant colonel

1939, December, leaves the Philippines

1941, September 29, promoted to brigadier general

1942, made assistant chief of staff under Chief of Staff General George C. Marshall

1942, March 27, promoted to major general

1942, May, named commmander of U.S. forces, European Theater of Operations

1942, November, chosen for Allied Forces Commander-in-Chief, North Africa

1943, February, made general (4 stars)

1943, July, invades Sicily

1943, September, invades Italian mainland

1943, December, chosen as Supreme Commander of Allied Expeditionary Forces

1944, June 6, Normandy invasion begins

1944, October, France liberated

U.S. presidents receive many wonderful, often strange, gifts. Because of his world fame and admiration, Eisenhower received one of the most interesting assortment of gifts, which by law must be turned over to the nation. Most of these have been assembled at the Eisenhower center at Abiline, including this magnificent inlaid desk, gift of the Shah of Iran.

1944, December 20, promoted to General of the Army (5 stars)

1945, March 7, bridge at Remagen captured intact

1945, April 11, U.S. forces reach Elba River, ordered to wait for Russians

1945, April 23, Red army enters Berlin

1945, April 25, American and Russian forces meet at the Elbe River

1945, May 2, Berlin surrenders to Russians

1945, May 7, Germany surrenders to Allies

1945, May 8, appointed Military Governor, U.S. Occupied Zone

1945, May 9, Soviets enter Prague, Czechoslovakia

1945, November 19, Ike made Chief of Staff of U.S. Army

1948, June 7, becomes President of Columbia University

1950, December 16, becomes first commander of the North Atlantic Treaty Organization (NATO)

1953, January 20, takes office as President of the United States

Outside the presidential library at the Eisenhower center stands this striking statue of the late general/president.

1953, July, Korean armistice proclaimed

1955, September, attack of coronary thrombosis

1956, November, again defeats Adlai Stevenson for presidency

1956, September, sends troops to Little Rock, Arkansas

1961, January 20, leaves presidency

1961, March, returned to active duty by order of Congress, signed by President Kennedy, with rank of General of the Army from December, 1944

1962, May 2, Eisenhower Presidential Library dedicated at Abilene, Kansas

1963-1965, memoirs published

1969, March 28, Dwight D. Eisenhower is dead at the age of seventy-nine

Opposite, As dusk darkens, visitors outside the Place of Meditation, where Dwight D. and Mamie Eisenhower are buried, are apt to recall the twilight days of the humble Abilene man who became a world leader and the confidant of world leaders.

THE GUILDHALL ADDRESS
June 12, 1945
By General of the Army Dwight David Eisenhower

Author's Note: This speech (courtesy of the Eisenhower Library) is considered one of the most notable of the time.

The high sense of distinction I feel in receiving this great honor from the City of London is inescapably mingled with feelings of profound sadness. All of us must always regret that your great country and mine were ever faced with the tragic situation that compelled the appointment of an Allied Commander-in-Chief, the capacity in which I have just been so extravagantly commended.

Humility must always be the portion of any man who receives acclaim earned in blood of his followers and sacrifices of his friends.

Conceivably a commander may have been professionally superior. He may have given everything of his heart and mind to meet the spiritual and physical needs of his comrades. He may have written a chapter that will flow forever in the pages of military history.

Still, even such a man—if he existed— would

Ike admired Lincoln, and they had much in common. Lincoln's Gettysburg Address is, perhaps, the best known of all time, and the Guildhall Address by Eisenhower, quoted here, is also one of the most frequently quoted. Ike expressed his appreciation for Lincoln by painting this portrait of the Great Emancipator.

sadly face the facts that his honors cannot hide in his memories the crosses marking the resting places of the dead. They cannot soothe the anguish of the widow or the orphan whose husband or father will not return.

The only attitude in which a commander may with satisfaction receive the tributes of his friends is in the humble acknowledgment that no matter how unworthy he may be, his position is the symbol of great human forces that have labored arduously and successfully for a righteous cause. Unless he feels this symbolism and this rightness in what he has tried to do, then he is disregardful of courage, fortitude, and devotion of the vast multitudes he has been honored to command. If all Allied men and women that have served with me in this war can only know that it is they whom this august body is really honoring today, then indeed I will be content.

This feeling of humility cannot erase of course my great pride in being tendered the freedom of London. I am not a native of this land. I come from the very heart of America. In the superficial aspects by which we ordinarily recognize family relationships, the town where I was born and the one where I was reared are far separated from this great city. Abilene, Kansas, and Denison, Texas, would together equal in size, possibly one five-hundredth of a part of great London.

By your standards those towns are young, without your aged traditions that carry the roots of

London back into the uncertainties of unrecorded history. To those people I am proud to belong.

But I find myself today five thousand miles from that countryside, the honored guest of a city whose name stands for grandeur and size throughout the world. Hardly would it seem possible for the London Council to have gone farther afield to find a man to honor with its priceless gift of token citizenship.

Yet kinship among nations is not determined in such measurements as proximity, size, and age. Rather we should turn to those inner things—call them what you will—I mean those intangibles that are the real treasures free men possess.

To preserve his freedom of worship, his equality before the law, his liberty to speak and act as he sees fit, subject only to provisions that he trespass not upon similar rights of others—a Londoner will fight. So will a citizen of Abilene.

When we consider these things, then the valley of the Thames draws closer to the farms of Kansas and the plains of Texas.

To my mind it is clear that when two peoples will face the tragedies of war to defend the same spiritual values, the same treasured rights, then in the deepest sense those two are truly related. So even as I proclaim my undying Americanism, I am bold enough and exceedingly proud to claim the basis of kinship to you of London.

And what man who has followed the history of this war could fail to experience an inspiration from the example of this city?

When the British Empire stood—alone but unconquered, almost naked but unafraid—to defy the Hitler hordes, it was on this devoted city that the first terroristic blows were launched.

Five years and eight months of war, much of it on the actual battle-line, blitzes big and little, flying V-bombs—all of them you took in your stride. You worked, and from your needed efforts you would not be deterred. You carried on, and from your midst arose no cry for mercy, no wail of defeat. The Battle of Britain will take its place as another of your deathless traditions. And your faith and endurance have finally been rewarded.

You had been more than two years in war when Americans in numbers began swarming into your country. Most were mentally unprepared for the realities of war—especially as waged by the Nazis. Others believed that the tales of British sacrifice had been exaggerated. Still others failed to recognize the difficulties of the task ahead.

All such doubts, questions, and complacencies could not endure a single casual tour through your scarred streets and avenues. With awe our men gazed upon the empty spaces where once had stood buildings erected by the toil and sweat of peaceful folk. Our eyes rounded as we saw your women, serving quietly and efficiently in almost every kind of war effort, even with flak batteries. We became accustomed to the warning sirens which seemed to compel from the native Londoner not even a single hurried step. Gradually we drew closer together until we became true partners in war.

In London my associates and I planned two great expeditions—that to invade the Mediterranean and later that to cross the Channel.

London's hospitality to Americans, the good-humored acceptance of the added inconvenience we brought, her example of fortitude and quiet confidence in the final outcome—all these helped to make the Supreme Headquarters of the two Allied expeditions the smooth-working organizations they became. They were composed of chosen representatives of two proud and independent peoples, each noted for its initiative and for its satisfaction with its own customs, manners, and methods. Many feared that those representatives could never combine together in an efficient fashion to solve the complex problems presented by modern war.

I hope you believe we proved the doubters wrong. And, moreover, I hold that we proved this point not only for war—we proved it can always be done by our two peoples, provided only that both show the same good-will, the same forbearance, the same objective attitude that the British and Americans so amply demonstrated in the nearly three years of bitter campaigning.

No man alone could have brought about this result. Had I possessed the military skill of a Marlborough, the wisdom of Solomon, the understanding of Lincoln, I still would have been helpless without the loyalty, vision, and generosity of thousands upon thousands of British and Americans.

Some of them were my companions in the High Command. Many were enlisted men and junior officers carrying the fierce brunt of battle, and many others were back in the United States and here in Great Britain in London.

Moreover, back of us always were our great national war leaders and their civil and military staffs that supported and encouraged us through every trial, every test. The whole was one great team. I know that on this special occasion three million American men and women serving in the Allied Expeditionary Force would want me to pay a tribute of admiration, respect, and affection to their British comrades of this war.

My most cherished hope is that after Japan joins the Nazis in utter defeat, neither my country nor yours need ever again summon its sons and daughters from their peaceful pursuits to face the tragedies of battle. But—a fact important for both of us to remember—neither London nor Abilene, sisters under the skin, will sell her birthright for physical safety, her liberty for mere existence.

No petty differences in the world of trade, traditions, or national pride should ever blind us to our identities in priceless values.

If we keep our eyes on this guidepost, then no difficulties along our path of mutual cooperation can ever be insurmountable. Moreover, when this truth has permeated to the remotest hamlet and heart of all peoples, then indeed may we beat our swords into plowshares and all nations can enjoy the fruitfulness of the earth.

My Lord Mayor, I thank you once again for an honor to me and to the American forces that will remain one of the proudest in my memories.

SOME SOURCES OF FURTHER INFORMATION

Dwight D. Eisenhower,
At Ease: Stories I tell to Friends **(1981)**
—Eastern Acorn Press (paper)
Mandate for Change **(1965)**
Waging Peace
Adams, Sherman
Firsthand Report: The Story of the Eisenhower Administration **(1970)**
Ambrose, S.E.,
The Supreme Commander **(1970)**
Ike: Abilene to Berlin **(1973)**
Sixsmith, E.K.G.
Eisenhower as a Military Commander **(1973)**
Eisenhower papers, edited by A.D. Chandler, Jr. and S.E. Ambrose (1970, five volumes)
Biographies
Larson, Arthur (1968)—Parmet, H.S. (1972)
Lyon, Peter (1974)

INDEX

ACKNOWLEDGMENTS

Dwight D. Eisenhower Library, Abilene Kansas, 2-3, 12, 14, 16, 23, 63, 84, 86-87, 89, 91, 93, 95, 97, 99, 101 Dwight D. Eisenhower Library, Audio Visual Department, 20-21, 36, 55, 58, 68, 70-71, 74, 76-77, 79, 80, 82, Dwight D. Eisenhower Museum, Abilene Kansas, 27, 42, 60, 65 Kansas Dept. of Economic Development, 10